# FROM TIME TO TIME

# FROM TIME TO TIME

*SELECTED POEMS*

## WILLIAM MONTGOMERIE

*In my beginning is my end . . .*
*. . . In my end is my beginning*
T.S. Eliot

*Para explicar mis problemas*
*le hablaré de geografía*
Pablo Neruda

CANONGATE
1985

First published in 1985
by Canongate Publishing Ltd
17 Jeffrey Street, Edinburgh

*The publishers acknowledge the financial assistance
of the Scottish Arts Council in the
publication of this volume*

*Cover photograph by Anthony Martin*

British Library Cataloguing in Publication Data
Montgomerie, William
From time to time.
I. Title
821'.914   PR6063.05/

ISBN 0–86241–078–9
ISBN 0–86241–079–7 Pbk

Typeset by Witwell Ltd, Liverpool
Printed and bound by
Clark Constable Ltd, Edinburgh, London, Melbourne

# CONTENTS

*To Norah*

I

# Aunt Zoë

Long ago
long before you were born
Uncle John brought his bride home
from England
that foreign country to the south
where father had never been

In the front room
she leans lightly
on her elegant long umbrella
mother's is black and useful
with a curved handle

I stare out of my shyness
at her hat
cartwheels rattle on granite
down Dalmarnock Street
mother's hatpins have black beads
not butterflies
and she pulls her hat on

Under her veil
my new aunt kisses mother
shakes hands with my father and
from a silver box
gives me a speck of menthol
that burns my tongue

She never sits down
stands there
leaning lightly
the last flounce of her skirt
on our flowered linoleum

From the height of her tiny waist
I am still staring at
the toe of her red shoe

## Ma Faither

Oors efter the schule skails
ma faither walks in at the tap o the street
Aye frae the same tramcaur frae the toon

in ae haun his tinned piece-box
in it his tea-an-sugar tin rattlin
an whiles his last piece
bramble jeely oozin through the yeast-holes
flavoured frae the newspaper wrappin

Walkin hame bi his side
A eat the piece

He races me up six flichts tae the door
cawin doon tae me
'Some day sonny you'll win'

At high tea he talks aboot the day
an his fella-journeymen
an the problem o pastin patches
on patterned wa-paper roon a gas-bracket
an hoo tae draw an ellipse on a ceilin
learnin us trade-secrets as
hoo tae lock a door wi nae key
hoo tae clean paper wi white breid

singin whiles an Irish folksang

He inventit a new lock wi a hinged key
unlike ony key A'd ever seen
makin the hoose-door burglar-proof
no that there's muckle worth stealin

Efter tea
he apens a flat parcel frae his pooch
an lays three scraps o papier-mâché
on the bare kitchen table

In a bowl he sturs floor an watter
trims the three grey scraps
wi lang paper-hingers' shears ▪

He pastes the embossed symbols
eidently on the flat stane
ablow the mantelpiece

Yin
an anchor wi chain
is Faith
twa
a blinfauld face
is Hope
three
a bird staunin on her nest
feedin her chuckens frae her ain flesh
the Pelican
is Charity

Faither
waitin ae day
till the paste is dry
paints the hale mantelpiece white

The three symbols
embossed on the flat surface
become yin wi the stane mantelpiece

★      ★      ★

Mony years later
A clamb the same stair
five flichts
tae the tap staircase winnock
apened it
tae luik doon on the backgreen
whaur A yinst played as a wean

Oor auld hoose-door
wi a different nameplate
apened
an an auld wife luikit doon
'A wiz boarn in that hoose' A said
hopin A micht be invitit in
an luik at the mantelpiece

'That wiz a lang time syne'
said the auld wife
an slammed oor hoose-door
shut

*Parkheid Cross (Glesca)*

# Breaking of Bread

As the church bells lull over Glasgow
we take the Black Book and our souls
sealed in envelope addressed to Hell
by God's predestinate hand and pen
through the stale close
past the pipeclayed tenement stair

This first morning of the week
as every first day of the week
in the Gospel Hall behind the tenements
bread and wine of the Last Supper
are laid again on clean linen

The Brethren and their Sisters
in Christ the Lord
foursquare round the table
meditate eternity in time
tired hands folded
Sunday-sundered from sound of the boiler-shop
from ship-rivetters in river yards
from yardstick and smell of the small draper's
from draped dummies in warehouse windows
from sins of Saturday sitting in cinemas
pipe and paper bet and bottle
sins
the ten sins of Sinai
sins of dim tenement closes
of parks in darkness
and lonely lanes

A Brother in black prays to God
in His armchair above the ceiling
Grandpa God's horn spoon
pauses between two bowls
of plain porridge and sour milk
with a small pinch from the salt cellar
as He listens to this one prayer
rising in the words of His own Book

Brother Tom
eardrums broken in a Clyde shipyard
retells Luke's tale
of Lazarus carried by God's angels
to Abraham's bosom

He calls across the great gulf fixed
between his two deaf ears and the World
to his son unsaved in the sinners' seat

Between us and you
father!
between your sons in the separate seats
and our father and mother among the Saints
are Luke's three yards of floor
and a deer-fence of iron air

Also between us and you
setting father at variance with son
Matthew's two-edged sword

Beside me brother John with head bowed
reads *The Treasure of the Incas*
between the last page of Revelation
and the back covers of his Black Book

At eleven o'clock always at eleven
grandfather looks at the round clock
on the whitewashed wall
then at the watch from his vest pocket
then at two overseers
checking the time from their vest pockets
they nod but no one moves

One says 'Amen!' and sighs
but no one moves
the women wait

A minute to eleven
grandfather walks to the table

   'That clock's a minute slow'

Father knows every text
from Genesis to Revelation
yet never says why the Last Supper
must be always at eleven o'clock

Grandfather lifts the plate
with the small loaf
thanks God and invokes his Brethren

   'Take eat
   this is my body which is broken for you
   this do in remembrance of me'

He breaks bread neatly
carries the plate two yards
proudly to the end of the front row
to his son our father who one day
hopes to carry the broken bread
to us his sons
and the Christian names of our children
will be the names of *his* family

The Elect are very few in the world
From Brother to Brother to Sisters
the plate passes in fellowship
from hand to hand from row to row
round the closed square to grandfather
who last pinches an inch off the dry bread
and thrusts it through his tea-stained white moustache

A moment to meditate the Mystery

From the second row of the sinners' seats
having again read the text
on the scroll beyond the wall clock

   For God so loved the world...
            John III 16

together we watch the cover glass
sweat over the wine
and drip
twice every weary hour

   'After the same manner also he took the cup'

says grandfather
lifting the little pane of glass
damp from the full winecup

'this cup is the new testament in my blood'

With two fingers
he lifts his moustache from his white beard
and drinks
not too deep
a demon sleeps in the red wine
of Christ's blood

Sister Mary
whose seat is vacant at the Lord's table
seen entering a pub will be visited
in her home by two overseers
and interviewed

Father takes from grandfather
the glass in both palms
drinks and hands it
with closed eyes contemplating death
Mother in a back seat sits
separate with her Sisters

In silence
the sound of coal burning in the black stove
a child running over a skylight
a dog barking somewhere in the world

   'Let's go to-night
   and switch the lights off at the dentist's!'

whispers John

We sit quietly two brothers
contemplating the switch-box
in the close in Westmuir Street
and the sudden darkness of Judgment Day
in all the houses up the stair

    'Hymn one-five-six
    beginning with the chorus!'

says grandfather

Happy voices of Brethren and Sisters
rise through the ventilators to Heaven

    'Christ is risen Hallelujah!
    gladness fills the world to-day
    from the tomb that will not hold Him
    see the stone is rolled away'

      ★       ★       ★

From the street behind the Colosseum
I take the Via Appia bus
through the Porta San Sebastiano
to the terminus

    '*Le Catacombe Signor!*'

says the conductor pointing through the close
between the green and red carboys
at the chemist's and the stale smell of the butcher's
to the Gospel Hall behind the tenements

# The Cross at Parkheid

A miner blue-scarred leashes his whippet
to the railings by the blue police-box

On the street skylight over the lavatory
the Close Brethren stand
in a ring round holy ground

A lightning conductor from Heaven
charging the little band with power
a Brother prays

   'Let Glasgow flourish
   by the preaching of the Word
   and the praising of Thy name'

The prayer dies under steel wheels
loud on tramlines of the double-decker
from Tollcross
that stops by the shut greengrocer's

Some leave clutching the brass rod
step up
go inside
climb upstairs
stand on the platform

The tramcar leaves for Glasgow Cross

   'Eternity! Eternity!
   Where will you spend eternity?'

The singing dies away

## Death and Resurrection

Eight o'clock
the last Brother from late work
hangs his black hat by the door
joins his bowed Brethren in silent prayer
Sisters with hands folded
children with wide eyes

The new Brother gone to his anteroom
his father in shirt sleeves
and long thigh boots
waits on the steps of the deep tank

Before the whole assembly
he speaks thus to the Brethren

    'A prayer heard on its way to God
    a preacher's word bounced from a stone tenement
    a hymn sung at a place where five roads meet
    are God's accidents
    designed from the first day
    to bring souls to this grave for burial
    to this tomb for resurrection

    'Salvation is God's lightning that strikes
    once in time in one place
    which is death burial resurrection
    of which baptism
    named by a word scholars have not translated
    is the sign

'Let us sing together
the first four verses of Hymn 3 – 4 – 0

"Is it Thy will that I should be
buried in symbol Lord with Thee?"'

Grandfather by the tank
watches the water

The new Brother in white
down three steps slowly    .
with him enters the dark water

'In the name of the Father
and of the Son
and of the Holy Ghost'

Grandfather lowers his son and Brother
into the dead water

Ripples over mouth nostrils shut eyes
waterweed hair awash
shoulders held
raised he rises reborn
on the top step stops
palms back his wet hair
dripping
blesses us with two arms
sings

'Up from the grave He arose
with a mighty triumph o'er His foes'

in a voice that lifts the whole hall

The new Brother
damp hair combed
sits by the hot stove
searches his *Believers' Hymnbook*
in self-confidence smiles
stands up

> 'Hymn 13
> Around Thy grave Lord Jesus
> thine empty grave we stand'

The Hall-door creaks open with a cold draught
stays open

In the close a child's laughter runs away

## Little Devil Doubt

Someone who became me
a schoolboy with the same name
in a railed green with no gate
found a dead cottage
but and ben with no roof
cement soft between the stones and
wall by wall
laid stones in loose heaps

and in the same way laid low
the prison-cell walls of Genesis stone by stone
stone by stone

Jehovah had not read Copernic's new book
so the twin Sun and Moon were born
one day after the flat earth

One star *epsilon Aurigae*
would fill Saturn's orbit and
between waters and waters
steam-cook the firmament
yet God wrote in His own Book
that He put all the stars there
in the firmament between the two waters

I watched Noah Shem Ham and Japheth
in the Ark with their four wives
clean out 8,000 bird cages
with new water birdseed an octopus bone
and sunflower seeds for the parrots
by day in a flutter of 24,000 butterflies
and by night 240,000 moths
in the men's beards in the women's hair for
40 nights 40 days and
150 days
while floodwaters prevailed on the earth

# Celtic Crowd

Yesterday from Saturday's match
grey bonnets flowed flooding Dalmarnock Street
five feet deep
over pavement road pavement
tenement to tenement close to close
to the tramstop by the pieshop
the stop by the fruitshop
for stops beyond Janefield
the tram by the grocer's
for stops to Tollcross
the Duke Street tram
by Garroway's Chemicals and the tannery
to closes in Dennistoun
the stop for Westmuir tenements
Shettleston Baillieston
for high tea

with pink sports editions
in the four pubs at every crossroads

till upstairs in a tramcar
from London Road to Parkhead Cross

'Fares!'

'That goal the day wiz affside'

'It wizny!'

'It wiz!'

'Fares!'

'It wiz nut!'

'It wiz sut!'

'C'mon lads
Feenish it in a backgreen!
Fares!'

# The Factor's

This shop with no window display
holds no stock
sells nothing
whose yashmaked face with no eyes
sees nothing
gives nothing to the street
is a square box for soiled notes
rubbed shillings
rent

From behind the counter the clerk gives receipts
in the back-shop the factor tots the ledger

'Rent!' says the cobbler
'that's three things
rent for a but-an-ben
twa rooms a box-bed in each
an aff the kitchen a scullery for jawbox an coal-bunker

'some hae a single-end and
nae ben-the-hoose
an a closet on the staircase

'an feu-duty! pennies in the week's rent
pey St George tae fecht the green dragon
though it deed langsyne

'St George o the land under the tenements
is noo the green dragon

'That's economics in a fairytale

'We hae nae use for this bug
under a plack or ahint the wa'-paper'

'He's daft!' say the neighbours
'the damned reid socialist!'

*Two Rhymes*
*from*
*Des Knaben Wunderhorn*

Quivit quaevit
the deuks a' gang barefit
the geese's feet are wat
Whit dae the wee hens think o that?

An whan A cam tae the Irish Sea
A fund three men an mair than three
the tane had naething ava
the tither had naething at a'
an the third had nocht

They coft a hapny bap
an a hunnerwecht o gusty cheese
an gaed wi't tae the Irish Sea

An whan they cam tae the Irish Sea
than they cam tae a toom toom land
a' banes an sand
an they cam tae a paper kirk
an a sandstane meenister coopit
in a wee ledder poopit
wha cried

    'We hae sinned the day
    gin God gie us life we'll aye dae sae'

An the three sisters o Lazarus
Catrina
Sybil
Stey still
grat bitterly
an the cock crawed buttermulk

2

The Scots Greys ride
sabres by their side

Cut the mannie's ear aff!
Na jist cut it near aff!

Lea a wee bit o his lug
an next time we'll ken the dog

*Princes Street (Edinburgh)*

## *Solemn Hour*
### by R. M. Rilke


Wha noo greets onywhaur i the warld
withoot cause greets i the warld
 greets ower me

Wha noo lauchs onywhaur i the nicht
withoot cause lauchs i the nicht
 lauchs me oot

Wha noo gaes onygate i the warld
withoot cause gaes i the warld
 gaes tae me

Wha noo dees onywhaur i the warld
withoot cause dees i the warld
 luiks at me

## Silver Eel

Ripples with tiny eyes
under a wave
leaves of waterglass
drift in the eye of the sun
by the warm Antilles
and cooling Atlantic Drift

Night under the floating forest
leaves them
drifts round the curve of yesterday
America slips down the west
beyond the Gulf Stream

Atlantic slides with them
down the dawn Galaxy
down the silver scroll
margined with constellations
to the end of a thousand nights
signed by the Hebrides
and brings these orphans
shrunk to little snakes
by Berneray
among the flotsam of the sea
washed by moontides
to this Gaelic estuary

Elder sister of these seaside infants
from midnight lochan
under the autumn Cuillins
pulled by inexorable lust
or life and death
held by the fishhook in her guts

on a line cast from Bermuda
on the south-west wind
drifting on ocean eddies
to this island
along the thread she spun of water once
from an egg under Sargasso
north-east by the Azores
by Rhum and Canna
to this little river

This silver eel
from under iron mountains
glides from her lochan spills downhill
over wet sphagnum
to where little trout with one red fin
hovering in deep pools
under waterfalls
rise to little flies and little hooks
to where the roadbridge
keyboard of loose planks under a holiday car
in low gear
is a hostel dance of hikers
in rubber soles
to where the river in spate
curls her tongue
a child with shut eyes
and licks deep
under a steep bank
to this estuary

Down a deep canyon
to the abysmal prairies
and plains of silt
beyond the Rockies of the mid-Atlantic ridges
her end seeks her beginning

*Skye*

27

II

## Sonnet After Silence

Were moon a month about this earth my nights
were world a year around the sun my days
of calendars
of diaries
seven flights of pigeons round the Kremlin
crimson rays seven of a star
eight from the Baltic out
is now a needle quivering on a chart
dog tail of earth
the circus roundabout
the shilling gyroscope that's come apart

Tongues swallow their serpent tails
and are nothing
windowless silence looks at the sky

In pencilled cobwebs
hung from star to star
the spiders of the constellations die

Within these sockets
where the eyes were dull
I twist a feather duster in a skull

# Rucksack

Five o'clock on a midwinter morning

Check the packed rucksack
ticking off the typed postcard
from the pocket
between emergency chocolate and
one-inch map!

Untie the top cord!
Wool-sweaters
vacuum flask of sweet tea
paper-wrapped ham- and jam-sandwiches
for the seat on snow
in lee of the top cairn

Retie!
Buckle the strap of the top flap
round the rolled oilskin!

Check the dry change in the suitcase!
Lock!

Compass into my breast pocket!

No nails loose on my climbing boots?
hob nails
steel tricounis
to grip not slip on iced rock
Knot the leather laces
over the ice-axe's steel pick!
and last
the brown balaclava

Pack the typed postcard for the next climb!

# To The Mountain

Boots and ice-axe balance the suitcase
as I leave the sleeping house
by the back stair
and Long Lane
a mile long they say
to the crossroads
where traffic lights wink all night
red amber green
to little traffic

Our coach waits
I hear her heart throb

Case and rucksack on the coat rack
ice-axe and nailed boots on the floor
I sit alone
too early for talking

Through a city asleep
till Sunday newspapers
and Sabbath congregations to kirk service
after a night of prowling street cats

By a numbered bus route
we leave the city
by market gardens
raspberry canes in rows
farms named at roads' ends
and country towns

The foothills close in
with tall firs
Gaelic birchtrees against a low sky

and the first white Bens
on the dawn horizon

I spread the one-inch map on my knees
find the five glens
and to-day's mountain
a mere Munro
timed between dawn and dark

The five Bens
four thousand feet and more
are for long Autumn days
or Spring
or week-ends
the Cuillins for Summer holidays

Off with my street shoes and town coat
I am water- and wind-proofed
over warm wool
up there
against ice-daggers at the heart

I don my clawed boots
to cling like an eagle
to iced crags
or wild cat to a tree

Maybe we'll climb where no stag goes

And last
my camera strap over one shoulder
the light-meter in one of my four pockets
my brown balaclava pulled over my ears
I climb down
leaving the warm coach
ice-axe at the ready as once a rifle

# The Mountain

At Loch Tay
Ben Lawyers rises
dark
into the grey sky of late winter
till
as we pass the village
the white mist rolls down the dark Ben
and rises again
on a snow-cemmed mountain

A party of five
we leave the hard road
for snowy heather
springy under our boots

Again
the mist like a tent
closes round us
shutting out the sky
and the mountain above us

At the first fork of a cold *allt*
we stop
under the mist dome
on a snow circle
turning our one-inch map
like a wheel
till compass-needle and longitude
are aligned

Next
a routine of every winter climb
we fill our boots with iced snow-bree
wading the right fork
to follow the left
pointing to the peak
our feet squelching in water
warming for the day

We climb
our first thousand feet
into the wind
that brings from higher up
the sound of cavalry
and out of distorting mist
goats dromedaries
horses lions
dragons
a herd of hinds
that pass us
to left and right
with the breeze that brought them
the scent of humans
and the clink of nailed boots

Sitting on our rucksacks
in the lee of the cairn
listening to the rattling call
of the white ptarmigan
and the grouse calling
'Go back! Go back! Go back!'
we tell stories of
mountain climbs in mist

## Footprints

I took my spring-day walk
from Coylumbridge
by forest paths
where roe-deer fled me
up through pine-forest
to the west ridge
spray blowing from the loch
a thousand feet up Coire na Caillich

I left my footprints
deep in snow
from Sgoran Dubh Mor
to Carn Ban Mor
when storm from the west
broke
with mist and snow

The shortest way down
was a thousand feet
to Loch Einich
a short-cut I began
step by step
kicked in frozen snow
till
remembering my son or daughter
due in May
I longed to see
I cut new steps
easier up than down
to the ridge I had left
now in thick fog
snow blowing level in the west wind

and on my right
yards away
a drop to death

I saw
like Friday's footprint in sand
my half-moon footprint in snow
and another and another
the heels downhill
my compass-needles home

Had I lived a hundred years ago
I would have knelt down
to thank God
for sending the west wind
to blow the snow
into one half only of my footprints

# *Mist*

In mist
we pegged our compass-reading
with three men in a straight line
and I as leader shouted
'Don't drift to the right!'

I looked back
to see the last man
out of line to the right
drop feet first
through the snow-cornice
down the cliff

Probing the snow
with long ice-axes
we found the cliff's edge
and looked down

The man was there
alive
standing on a ledge
twenty feet below

We dropped him a rope's end

# Spectre

On my Harzreise
between Schierke and Altenau
I climbed the Brocken in mist
and saw no spectre
and on the misty Bens of Cairngorm
or Grampians
no Grey Man of the Mountains

Once only
on a misty road in Angus
cycling into the low sunset
from Arbroath
a shadow giant on a shadow cycle
followed me
for a mile
dismounting as I dismounted
mounting his cycle as I mounted mine
and
as the sun set behind a cloud
he vanished

## Zircon

In the green brilliant I gave you An Lochan Uaine
from Ryvoan Pass
under the long screes of Craig nan Gall
hieroglyphs of pine and
from the Lairig
a gold eagle on a blue shield

Add this to the gem on your left hand
*Il Lago di Nemi*
green in the Alban Hills

On the Thieves' Road
the little Green Loch you loved
and carry for ever on your third finger
Hesper from a green sky
in the weme of the ring
is the love of firefly
glow-worm
Phoenix and Turtle burning in green fire
that glowed for Marja and Pierre in the Rue Lhomond

# En Una Noche Oscura
## (E.S.P.)

At midnight in black darkness
awake both in a still room in sleeping London
two watches
synchronised in seconds to the same pulsebeat
waiting yet unaware that we are waiting

Wrists and hearts and arteries
tick time timeless
our ears in silence resting
our eyes in darkness watching
awaiting
unaware of
out of silence out of darkness the lightning

Without light without thunder
it strikes
quiet as a bat passing
softly as the first light imagined
idea before creation
before the first word before the beginning

The opaque bone dividing
us brain from brain
mind from mind is
clear crystal
returning us the light of our eyes
there is no other
in this midnight without stars without moonlight

Vision of forms in silence
silent
as at midnight I look toward you
unseeing
and read eyeless
without print
without speaking
mind thinking in your dear head pillowed so near me

Translating the deep silence
I speak to your ears the live shapes of meaning
that break gently the quiet
surface we watch together
you at home in your mind I an incomer

A black lightning of panic
strikes without thunder and
from nowhere
gnosis
there is no cause for terror
as a high tide from ocean
washes in over us

A throne empty glows among the dark stars
and our firstborn unborn
dances with the Dancers
to the drums of our hearts
beating in quiet ecstacy to the music of silence

## Aunt Jeannie

You stare with the glass eyes of a doll
eyes that blink open
shut
open
that have looked on your man dying
your husband dead and coffined
chin propped on a black hymnbook

Between living and dying
only the breathing quilt and your tired eyes move
your mind having bat-flittered round the white ceiling's
                                                    cornice
and moled along the skirting
three sleepless nights and daylights
may die screaming

Tangled in the meshed birdnet
of space-time's four dimensions
only your wings free
beat with no progression
in this void with no vistas
in this now with no future
in this house with the door shut and blind windows

From the seventh dimension comes gnosis
gently I give you
my four fingers stroking your forehead
quietly I talk of now and tomorrow
of your daughters and sons
of your grandchildren with their sons and daughters

My fingers are his fingers
and my voice his voice speaking
of those children
his body's resurrection
You pass over the bridge of one hair
which is time future

I rise switch the light out and leave you sleeping

# Triptych of Miniatures

## I

### To the Dark Lady

Let me go then into those dark flowers
fall in long parabolas through black skies
over continents sliding to dawn and sunset
symbols of a world I hold in my hands and kiss

or in those dark eyes tunnel the Alps
from green Swiss valleys to long fields
in Lombardy
walk *nella Loggia della Signoria*
or Magna Graecia's temples with red oleanders.

But thin nebulae under dark eyelashes
are mist on white peaks in high passes
drifting over ricefields among windbreak
saplings shivering over frozen ditches.

The nebulae would flash jale gold ulfire
to stars did I know the word spoken in the beginning.

# II
## *Autolycus to Merope*

To-night this lift with automatic mind
counts 1 to 10
                    10 to 1
zero
    Sisyphus counts his ten fingers
or heaves his eternal punishment to the tenth floor.

Hermes my father taught me metamorphosis
I shall shape-shift you to Merope the Pleiad
Long ago the lift-man forgot you
his simple brain is wired to an electric main.

Shall we leave his lift or walk downstairs
unconsidered moments stolen from time
away from the taped music and chatter in the bar
long enough to say I love the laughter in your eyes?

Later between two dances shall we look at Orion
(framed in the window) chasing your six sisters?

# III

## *Fine Frenzy*

Do I dare disturb the universe?

I put a night square of darkness from Pegasus
in the typewriter
tap diamond Sirius
Mars the ruby
Vesper silver goddess
symbols of a mathematic beyond Einstein

Slipping the Great Dog I flush Capricornus
along a short-cut goatpath
that telescopes the universe to a yardstick
of space-time
a starred ellwand

That jewelled ell of three stars
is a child's ruler to measure infinities of indifference
I chuck it back into the dark attic of the sky

## Winter Solstice

The midwinter bee still in moss
dreams her first dim dream of Spring
Snowdrops stirring in cold soil
sing gold carols to God the Sun

Yasmin lifts yellow Iranian candles
Hellebore cups of rose and ivory
by night to Capricorn and the Three Kings
at chill dawn to the moonsilver Sun

Conceived in womb of the Spring Equinox
dying in resurrection born in death
the Sun of Mary sleeps in the sign of the Goat
at the gate of Janus in the arch of the New Year

The snail will unlock her door the bat wake
that sleeps with cobwebs and echoes of carols
in the chill barn
On silver twigs on the lintel
a death's head folds her moth wings

Loki flickers in the twilight of Tiw
in our pocket book of hours
Gods and Caesars
sleep in the new calendar and the month Mars
massacres innocents in all Bethlehems of the world

Sing rather the carol of Akenaten
to the newborn year
the Sun rising

# III

# Tay Estuary

The Law
holds
in a hollowed hand
hill and river
holds
to the far horizon
sky's blue bubble
turning

Orion turns
and the burning sun
round the Hill
and still Pole
turns
on the wheel of the world
turns the shape of the sky

Ships depart
blind lighthouses wait
pilot cutter
and little harbour lights
on a Ness in Angus
and the shadow of Fife

Red buoys tilt and turn in the estuary
for ships returning
held by hill and river
ships and sky
held by river and hill

# Broughty Wa's*

Fisher Street beyond the north wind
dozes a Hansa dream by the dead estuary

Broughty Walls guard no ballad
the song is a dead seagull on shingle

Glenhazlen's drowned and the fish that ate him
shoal elsewhere The fishermen listen to the radio

Burd Helen's buried without a grave
and maggots are under the seagull's wings

The lovers have forgotten one another
drowned and buried they have long forgotten themselves

The song has forgotten them the crabs taste it
at high tide and at low tide the flies

The Ship Inn drunk at half-past-nine
sings songs of the radio in Fisher Street

*The title of Child's ballad, Number 258

## Broughty Ferry

The lamps across the river
are lilies of light
rooted with fire

The evening star
is a windflower of light

The crescent moon
holds the apple of darkness
in a glass

Three fishermen
are talking by the drawn-up boats

They know the dark river
and the sea beyond

# Lifeboat

A cannon shot
outside
in the night cannot be target practice
from the fort by the castle

I run upstairs
to the attic window
overlooking the dark roofs
till
from the second maroon's cannon shot
in the sky
slowly a green star drifts down

The Coxwain
propping the first maroon
on the pebble beach
beyond the steps of the lifeboat shed
lit the short fuse
and stepped back
the first shot heard
from the height of the church clock
louder and further than
St Aidan's bell on Sunday

The second shot
heard and seen from windows in the fishing village
by pale faces
between parted curtains

Heavy boots
are running in Castle Street
and cars race west
on the esplanade

The slipway was oiled well on time
now the Coxwain greets
the last man of his crew
climbing the steps to the chained lifeboat
where the yellow oilskins hang high
like washing on a fishwife's kitchen pulley

The lifeboat shed opens
like a cachelot's mouth
(Broughty Ferry was once a whaling station)
the crew in oilskins and sou'westers
have climbed to their places
the Coxwain to his wheel

'Let's go!' he says

Unchained
the lifeboat moves
speeds up
like a skate on ice
down the slipway
ploughs the first wave in two
rises to the second
and fades to a throbbing searchlight
on the fairway
halfway across the estuary

I join the locals
old fishermen and commuters
from the constellated city
yonder
across the estuary
where flashing buoys
shout their names

in red and white seconds
on the black water
the Newsome the Middle bank
the Fowler Rock
and the red lights of the city riverfront

I move from group to group
gathering rumours
from the ship's radio
from the Coastguard's phone
and what the crewmen said as they passed

One old fisherman naming the buoys
the Lady the two Abertays
the two Middle Buoys
the two Outer
and talking of undercurrents
under tow
cross currents
ebb and flow of tides
eddies whirlpools
wash and backwash
tells us where drowned men finally lie

There is little else to do
than wait patiently
here in the cold night
or walk on the pier
waiting for the lifeboat's light
to cross the bar
or maybe I'll walk home to a warm bed
and read about it in
to-morrow morning's *Courier*

*Broughty Ferry*

*Lifeboat Disaster*
*(April 1960)*

*To James Coull, Coxwain*

> *Tween the Isle of May*
> *and the Links o Tay*
> *mony a ship's been cast awa*

Folkrhyme

Storm
from the North Sea's December
over St Andrews Bay
over eider muirs of Fife
and two miles of white estuary
north against this shore

Sand sifts out of the south
soft as blown mist over a muir
in headlights of motorcars
from this beach where
dunlins twittered all night
a flurry of fine sand
on the esplanade
a scurry of sand in a lane
drifting for a night
a day
and half a night
over roads
over pavements
over parapets into gardens

Sand and fine rain find
warped wood and weathering stone
finger a salt-rusted catch
find a draught in the window frame
spill an hourglass on the floor

All this second night
the wind drops slates into gardens
bends steel radio masts at the chimney
smashes their teeth on the slates

All night
a mad gate beats against a broken lock

We lean back
on the black wind
watch our footprints by the lamp
drift away in a mist of sand
and listen

Hours are blown with the rain
three oyster catchers flee over the wet slates
calling

A buoy flashes
red
in the fairway
to the four-mile faraway city
The Horseshoe counting
four-and-a dark seconds
flashes silver

Darkness the dragon has eaten the Lady
and a sea-mist the lightship
In the fairway by the Gaa Sands
black night the cormorant
shakes the third light
and swallows it
South-east by the Fife skerries
the North Carr rocks her crew
looses the cat-clawing anchor
drifts
eight men and a light
drifts and holds
on the last anchor

The first maroon knocks loudly
once
on the wet shutters of heaven
drops a green firefly
They wake in cottage bedrooms
open the curtain
watch the sky

Unchained
our lifeboat is loosed
to the indifferent sea
where storms
forecast from cottage radios
meet the timetable tide
beginning its slow ivy crawl
up wormcast beaches
up posts and harbour walls
washing the glass hands of barnacles

The lifeboat rolls
rises
dips
past the pilot's pier
(where in other midnights
the silver wash under the jetty
flickers on the black cutter's hull
going up
going down
in the lift of the tides)
past the swimming club
and the castle
(whose cannon once guarded the narrows
whose war rockets like two hands
ripped the canvas of the sky)

Forty horsepower under the floorboards
galloping
beat under the bootsoles of the crew
The coxwain defines his straight line
through the rain curtains and the mist drifting
and a lost gull silver in the searchlight

The coastguards watch from the two shores
the short waves talk to one another

  'Jist passin the Abertay lightship'

  'Jist approachin positions o the Middle Buoys'

  'The North Carr Lightship has fired
  a white flare
  Can ye see the flare?
  an gie me yer position!'

  'Aye we see that ane
  but we're no clear yet'

All night the short waves talk
to the silent dark
but the dark comprehends it not
nor the silence
round the last corner of time
for beyond the bar over the Gaa Sands
the Mona has rolled over her crew
Ronald Grant Coxwain and his seven
holding them under water
like a swan a duck
or a mother smothering her bairns
rolling over them
and lies mastless
a coffin on the beach
with seven drowned men
and a man missing

The plaque on the boathouse wall honours them

       ★      ★      ★

The weathercock on the kirk steeple
swings on the wind blowing
from the North Sea
from Fife
(the beggar's cloak with the fringe of gold)
from Atlantis and
in lee of the cold
five men turn in time with
the tail of the gold cock
All day by the lifeboat shed
they loiter by the steps
down to the pebble beach
or on the road by the dead men's plaque
or on the beach sand
out of the west wind

Here is the sump for whalers' tales told
in the Ship Inn bar
sailors' tales
war tales I shall tell elsewhere
lifeboat tales and
scraps of newspaper
blown down Fort Street to the boathouse

'Whit wey wiz the boathook lashed tae the wheel?
an the engineroom hatch open
that midnicht tae wind an watter?
an the droont mechanic halfwey tae the engine?'

They quiz the Inquisitor's verdict
the lifeboat Mona guilty of witchcraft
having said nothing in her own defence
handed over to the secular arm for burning
in another place to avoid local disturbance

I have stood by you
Coxwain James Coull
at your wheel
your two hands relaxed
your knees lax
would tense like a boxer's
when the feint and the knock-out come together
when the feint and the knock-out were two waves
almost together
countered on the wheel
by your hair-trigger fingertips
ere your brain knew
a skill coiled and oiled
in hands and arms
in thirty storms in twenty-five years

that brought a hundred lives and more
ashore
to hot tea and baps in the kirk hall
a skill not to be learned in five weeks

I am remembering a dozen heroes who harried Hell
beginning with Orpheus who went to Hades
to bring back Euridice his wife
(one life)
and failed

You
Coxwain
went thirty times into chaos
and came home with a hundred lives

From Theseus in the Labyrinth
killing the Minotaur
bull-headed son of the white bull
and nymphomaniac Pasiphae
I turn to
a live black bull
an earthquake shaking the ground
to Ordoñez the bullfighter
between two horns nagging Death
killing
with a surgeon's skill between the shoulder blades
and from him to this quiet man
facing the bull of the sea bellowing against the land
from the cold labyrinth of waves and wind
where underfoot moves in three dimensions

from the myths of death
to the truth of death

The five men by the lifeboat station
have watched you pass along Fisher Street
like Dante from Hell
scorched by your lifeboat burning

*Broughty Ferry*

# IV

# Berlin

On my first full salary I sailed from Leith
to Hamburg my first foreign city

On the Berlin express I learned at lunch
to ply two forks for the fish course
and drank my first bottle of Rhine wine

Dear Mother
                    I am writing this in my room
in Berlin-Karlshorst at a great desk
with tooled leather folders and inkstand
of solid silver

The late Herr Busch
left a daughter and this town flat
to his widow
after his fortune inflated and burst
and a vein in his brain broke

My room rent is twelve marks a week

The coffee-grinder in the kitchen and a morning knock
bring widow-Busch with '*Guten Morgen*'
coffee rolls and butter on a tray at eight

The lime leaves in Prinz Adalbert Strasse
filter the hot sun flickering green
on my white marble Venus
on my white shutters
with Herr Busch's boxing gloves on a nail

The great city's a map on the cleared desk

## Die Mensur

First
looking upstreet and down
you knock at an anonymous door
and upstairs
past the bar
with *Bier Mittagessen*
*Suppe Fleisch Gemüse*
we walk into
the hot tobacco mist of the *Mensur*

As if for inspection
your corps brothers line up
bowing each from the waist

   *'Sehr angenehm!'*

Along the long line
I bow from the waist

   *'Sehr angenehm! Sehr angenehm!'*

We watch the rites
of this secret mystery
they say is illegal

The look-out watches from his little window

First
two *Paukante*
face to face
sword to sword
a sword's length between them
necks bound
right arms bandaged
hands in the hollow hilts
their *Sekundante* crouching
swords at rest

   '*Mensur fertig! Los!*'

The two *Paukante* raise swords
in defence of the left cheek
slash down in attack
in this strange duel of swords and faces
like two mechanical bell-ringers
striking hours
on a town clock

Gold sparks fall
through the thin fog

In the blond hair of one head
the blood clots
drips to the neck
to the white trousers
to the floor

The two *Sekundante* raise swords
to still
the anvil hammering of ringing steel

The wounded man
removing his red goggles
stares with great white eyes
in a wet red face

The *Testant*
with dipped cotton wool
washes his wound
and swabs the two swords

Again and again
the same pattern repeats

They stroke their corps ribbons
from right shoulder to left hip
then in the bar
where they drink no alcohol
show me how they heaped their corps caps and
drove one sword through all of them
binding the Brotherhood

When the first man joins us
in new white turban
they show me their old scars
a half-healed wound in a shaved scalp
a wide slash down a left cheek
like Iron-Cross ribbons first-class

*Berlin*

Mensur: students' duel Bier: beer Mittagessen: lunch Suppe: soup Fleisch:
meat Gemüse: vegetables Sehr Angenehm!: very welcome! Paukante:
duelling students Sekundante: seconds Mensur fertig! Los!: Duel ready!
Go! Testant: attendant with antiseptic

# *War*

'It's begun!'
I say to the man on the Broughty bus

'What's begun?'

'The war
Warsaw's been bombed'

'Who bombed it?'

'The Germans I suppose'

'That's funny
Warsaw's the capital of Russia'

'No!
Warsaw's the capital of Poland'

'Oh!'

At home we hold each other
in silence
looking to the horizon
the North Sea
and Germany
remembering Italian mustard gas
sprayed on Abyssinians
Count Ciano's bomb
dropped on a circle of men
who opened like a rose
and the German Condor Legion
bombing Guernica
on market day

# The Edge Of The War
## (1939–)

On the esplanade
the deck-chair hirer
watches his summer
shovelled into sandbags
till at high tide
the beach is flooded to the Promenade

Our submarines like five alligators
pass
always at dusk
to the North Sea
where a German plane has sown surface mines

One mine circles the harbour slowly
missing the pier
again and again and again
until defused by a simple twist of the wrist

The whelk-seller leaves his bag and barrow
to pull a mine up the beach
and dies
'Stretchers! Stretchers here!'
they shout from the Castle

A policeman arrests one mine on the shore
and drags it halfway to the police-station
his tombstone a cottage gable-end
pocked with holes packed with red putty

Casks of brandy butter and ham
float on to the beach
from a mined ship

A grocer's van parks at dusk
by the Castle railings

Sergeant MacPherson pins on his notice-board
'Flotsam butter from the beach
must be left immediately
at the police-station'

For days the streets are sweet
with the smell of shortbread

Blue-mould butter
is dumped on the counter
or thrown at night
over the wall of the station
where greased door-handles will not turn

A German plane
following the wrong railway
dumps his bombs on an up-country farm

A plane from the North-Sea sunrise
machine-gunning our little fishing fleet
brushes a wing against a mast
and ditches

'*Hilfe! Hilfe!*'

'Take your time lads!'
shouts a skipper
to a drifter turning toward the sinking plane

'One of our planes
has sunk a German U-boat
off Montrose'

A war-rumour

The submarine
one of ours
dented
is in dry-dock
in Dundee

Bennet from Stratford-on-Avon
one of the crew
cycles to our house
with no lights
sings to us
of Boughton's Lordly Ones
from *The Immortal Hour*
talks of his wife in Stratford
and of the night they watched Birmingham burning

After late supper
he returns to the night
having left his ration of pipe-tobacco
on the piano

If his submarine sinks
he knows how to escape
and is found afloat
on the Pacific Ocean
drowned

On Tents Muir
across the Tay estuary
parachutes are falling
from war planes

We talk of the Second Front

One parachute does not open

*Broughty Ferry*

# Epitaph

*for 2nd Officer James S. Montgomerie of the S.S. Carsbreck,
torpedoed off Gibraltar, 24th October 1941*

My brother is skull and skeleton now
empty of mind behind the brow
in ribs and pelvis empty space
bone-naked without a face

On a draughty beach drifting sand
clawed by a dry skeleton hand
sifts in the hourglass of his head
time useless to bones of the dead

# Thirty Years After

When you woke in the dark
listening from your bunk
to the ship's heartbeat
what fears came to you
from a boy's Glasgow
drowned deep in a man's memory
under curved dolphins
wide-winged gannets
floating isles of blae jellyfish
sea-fog
time-fused fears
deeper than nerve-ends of feeling
by day
beyond red and violet
by night
between dream and dream
between wave-bands of the ship's radio?

Still Hell under the keel
waked to terror
in a U-boat's crab eye
a torpedo between two waves
a bomb from a child's Heaven
Death with a razor
in this dark lane
ten-miles-of-rain wide
between our wiped windscreen
here in Spain
and brown beaches and Moroccan white houses in Africa
where nor'-west
Nelson waited for Villeneuve
where *Unterseebooten*
that night waited

★　　　★　　　★

Father looked up
that October night
from his black Bible
marked the place with conference notes
laid Book and pen
on the kitchen fender

You said
'I know this is my last voyage'

'Let's pray!' said father
kneeling
elbows on his armchair

In the morning
you caught the first tramcar to Glasgow Docks
with a suitcase of clean underwear
and father's Bible

By divine telepathy listening in
God removed Hell
from under your keel
and in Heaven was joy
over one sinner repenting

In convoy by Land's End
by Finisterre
off duty you read your new Bible
between Cape St Vincent and Trafalgar
on the dark bridge hummed hymns
and timed the lighthouses

Here the nick-rhymed *S.S. Heartbreak*
broke
in a nightmare of decks tilting
alleyways at false angles
the rude sea entering all your exits

The dark night dipped you in baptism
in black water
with no blessing
in the name of Father Son Holy Ghost
no arm under your shoulder
in the Gospel Hall baptistry
no Brethren to sing resurrection

Only thanks from the Third Officer
for his life
and the crew rescued

Three bronze stars and silver medal
the bronze Atlantic Star
and Africa Star
the 1939–45 bronze star
the 1939–45 silver Medal
with bright ribbons in a brown cardboard box

but nothing for the life you gave
to save your crew

*Tarifa*

## Elegy For A Soldier
*for John Sinclair Montgomerie, Royal Artillery*
*16th May 1942*

One in a graveyard in a city of gravestones
in a city carved from a stone deathshead
is nothing now
under the cold bone of the moon
in the starred Sahara of midnight
nothing
the name of nothing

Here's a skull now
*und niemand kann die dürre Schale lieben*

Nothing has no body
nor any shadow
the shadow of nothing has no surname
the name of them who buried nothing here
and carried home a shadow among the shadows

We dropped a cold bone
into the ground
and raised a stone
quarried and carved from the world
silver skull of the moon's midnight

The moon has dead eyes
in a night of microbes

## The Man With One Arm

Finishing Brecht's last sentence
*Die Hand hoch*
*der gefürchtete SS-Mann*
I lay his poem face downward
remembering my pen-pal
Gerhard who died later on the Russian front

and his widow who lives
at the same address beyond the Berlin wall
in a side street with her son
and my only two brothers
whose daylight died under earth under water

Multiply by some millions!

Then one day south of the Brenner
in August
the white Ötztaler Alpen
the sun on a meadow where
a peasant whetting his scythe watches us

In the inn yard you lift
your face with eyes shut to the afternoon sun
and I on the *Gasthaus* bench
in twelve inches of shadow
slake from a tall glass five hours of burning sky

An unshaven tramp shares my bench
and in German we talk cities
Rome Moscow
he had not seen the Red Square
Lenin's tomb nor St Basil's
Moscow without Lenin and that endless queue!

I fill his empty beerglass
'And Stalingrad!
Had you not noticed?' says he
patting his left shoulder and empty sleeve
'What waste of men and materiel!'
My mirror asks no questions

He brings a full bottle
fills my glass
talks of his farm and his two sons
one in Roma one in Wien
Were they taught how in London
old Sterzing was rebaptised Vipiteno?*

A question I do not ask
many questions I have not asked
but listen
how his cows go to pasture
when the sun over the ridge
lifts the shadow and night-dew from his meadow

His sawn winter logs are piled by the outhouse
his new hay heaved to the loft
his oats cut
potatoes stored
roof mended
  *'Wir sind bereit!'*
He looks north to the snowfields of the high Alps

    Eyes under a steel helmet
behind a machine-gun have become peasant
talking Tiroler to peasant
We shake hands across Europe
and across many frontiers

*Trentino (S. Tirol)*

*By the secret Treaty of London (26th April 1915), Britain and her allies promised Italy a large bribe of territory, including German-speaking, Austrian South Tirol, if Italy joined the Allies within one month. South Tirol, south of the Brenner, is still in Italy. We heard rumours of bombs in the valleys.

## Elegy
### for William Soutar
#### Poet
#### (1898 – 1943)

A narrowing of knowledge to one window
to a door swinging inward
on a man in a windless room
on a man inwardly singing
on a singing child
alone and never alone
a lonely child
singing
in a mirror dancing to a dancing child
memory sang
and words in a mimic dance
old words were young
and a child sang

A narrowing of knowledge to one room
to a doorway
to a door in a wall
swinging
bringing him friends
a narrowing of knowledge to
an arrow in bone in the marrow
an arrow
death
strung on the string of the spine

To live crystal in the palm
and the five fingers
to the slow thirty years' pearl in the hand
shelled in a skull
in the live face of a statue
sea-flowered on the neck of broken marble
sunk fourteen years in that aquarium

# Saint Valentine's Day

This clear morning let's walk in Rome
together you and I
crossing the *Piazza Flaminia* at the green light
*Avanti!*
careful of the cars at the *Porta San Valentino*

In the Pincio Gardens
we'll watch *Pulcinella*
and the demon corbies kissing at Nero's tomb

They say the Saint's remains are at *San Prassede's*
here by the Railway Terminal

This afternoon
let's take the *Metropolitana*
past the square Colosseum of the twenty-year empire
to *Ostia Antica*

In the house of Amor and Psyche
I'll share with you
my love
their divine kiss of two millennia
in its box of Roman brick and white marble
set in blue sky

V

## Christmas Eve

No dog no cat moves
on the chill promenade

On tiled pavements
under white hotels
chill chairs with naked legs
stand round bare table

In constellations
the bombs hang
over the black Mediterranean

Over our heads
the stars in rockets are
footnotes to Genesis
and Revelation

Aldebaran on the brow of *Toro*
Orion the matador with sword
and Sirius barking all night
with the wild dogs

*Fuengirola*

# Moonfade

Tu en as assez de vivre dans l'antiquité grecque et romain
*Apollinaire*

Grey swell from the black Mediterranean
undercut leans over
shatters the moon to quicksilver
and white froth on brown sand

I turn from the north star
over the *Sierra de Mijas*
calling the moon Isis
and the morning star Astarte

I've watched with millions
a man's boots walk on Diana's bow
and await the last analysis of Hecate's dust

Hercules walked this way west
from Urci by Malaga
to Gibraltar and Atlas

Ulysses sailed that sea
black now to the horizon
where dawn in the clear east
is a fever flush on a child's cheek
nailing his shields and ships' beaks
in Athene's temple
by the gold sands of Odysseia

Athene with Moors and Jews converted
is Virgin of the Martyrs

92

Beyond the gitana shanties
from the *Plaza Generalísimo Franco*
the church clock strikes eight

Slowly the still sea turns to the sun

The first sardine boat is
a red light moving over black water

The horizon slides down the sun

In line astern out of the burning sea
come masts of ebony
in a swarm of black gulls

It is day
without stars without planets
the silver paper of the moon's crescent
Isis
Diana
Hecate
burnt to white ash

*Fuengirola*

# Cockfight

Spain has closed two hands
thumb to thumb fingers to fingers
round this house on the hill
whose white walls crow
Christ denied

Matadors and prize cocks in gold frames
child barmaids serve Miguel beer and *tortillas*

From warm steps
we watch the blue Mediterranean
and talk of Pamplona bullfights
Berlin duels
young razor gangs in Glasgow

The two gates of the ring
shut
cocks in mid-air tear

A camera's one eye watches
punters watch
judges watch turning their sandglasses
*aficionados* light cigarettes

Fighting cocks must not fight to the death of a thousand cuts
but judges misjudge and
red life bubbles out of a
dead beak hanging

the champion chaired on red hands
round the arena

*Carvajal*

# Nerja Cave

For an hour let's leave earth
where the one-way metronome of the sun swings
from left to right over Africa
from winter rains to June solstice
keeping rhythm and life

to the halls of Hell
a sunless landscape without leaves
without flowers without birdsong
in jungles of stone not yet trees
a stone sky suspended
over a rock earth not yet world
whose stone pillars support nothing
a vast experiment with one element
in a laboratory with no scientist
whose waterclock drips limewater
on surfaces at many angles
every lime molecule a moment in time
hours years millennia millions of years
just short of eternity
short of the capital A of the Answer to no question
while years record for no one
layered teeth of time
in a stone mouth with no face

Walls leave fine dust on our fingertips
teeth splinter on rock fruit
we taste cold limestone
sniff grey roses

Bats flittering among echoes of gnat voices
listen to shapes of rocks in a night without stars
where
before the gods became God

before gods
stone organ pipes played silence to the dark

# El Chico

The navel of your world
Pepe!
is not where a paper map of Spain
poises on a pinpoint at Angel's Hill* but
in the *Mesón Canaleja* in *Jerez*
here

This Holy Week beginning
the glass door with typed menus
opens with a draught and soft sift of rain

Little Pepe!
unnoticed by Americans at the booked table
by wine porters clattering in out in
gulping *arguardiente* on the house
by *Madrileños* only the head waiter remembers
dusting old memories as *tapas* to dark brandy

Behind the tall bar
little Pepe with the white apron
you file paper napkins on wire
pack toothpicks in a pewter cup
wipe glasses
tuck the towel in your belt and
keep your place

*South of Madrid, the omphalos of Spain

aguardiente: spirits
madrilenos: native of Madrid

97

## Armadillo

Sailor!
the two bead eyes of your stuffed armadillo
watch three dawn caravels
sail from the pier palms of Palos
where Don Christopher Columbus
ferries Christ on his lateen shoulder


Stout Cortes with condor eyes
stares at Aztec Quaupopoca and all his men
at the stake burning
silent upon a square in Mexico


Saint Francis Pizarro
sells life to a hi-jacked Emperor
for a million times thirty pieces of silver
the silver double-cross of Father Vicente
sells waterdrops a cheap cord death and Heaven
to the chained Inca paying twice for nothing


Your stuffed armadillo within my skull
sailor!
in a child's voice sings

    The spirit says Come!
    and the bride says Come!
    and take the water of life freely

*Palos*

## Santa Filomena

So Gerald and Lynda left
for Greece and Turkey
down the long avenue
between the *Cañada de las Palomas*
and Gerald's olive grove

The car dipped
at the avenue's end
to the road
and was gone
for two long months and more
leaving us with the cat
the house
*Santa Filomena*
and the round rose-beds
in the olive grove

Every morning early
by the kitchen door
I switch on
well-spring water
from beyond the badger's sett
to the house arteries

Now
from the *mirador*
upstairs by the study
Carrington's *Wadentlath Farm*
in the room behind me
I taste the landscape
like a dry sherry

trying

so far in vain
to match names on the map
with those nameless white *pueblos*
yonder
set in green olive groves
and vineyards
snowed with almond blossom

Later
below the *terraza*
in scent of jasmine
in our cane chairs
the cat on a kitchen chair
we watch
the little events that make Spain

A herd of goats
weed the *Cañada*
or orchids
one that strays from the herd
brought to order
by a round pebble
from the boy David's sling

In the cool house
bluebottles buzz on the stair window

Between sun and shade
a carpenter bee
bounces from the room's shadow
and bumbles at the reed screen
over our parked car

Purple spiderwort
flutters on the brick steps

A flock of hammer-headed hoopoes
tintack a flowered rug
to hot earth

Bee-eaters juggle their long tails
on the high wire
below a falcon
half-dissolved in light
gliding in blue sky

Somewhere between the house and the forest
among olives and black almond trees
all day a cuckoo calls
and the hoopoes
Hoo-poo-poo!

Knobbed fig trees
with green hands
opening to the sun
beg pesetas of rain

All night
a fox-bark rings the house-cat
up an olive tree

This cat we feed
on raw fish
and milk from the market
brings a dead shrew
to our feet
claws a nestling in the grass
a lizard
to play with on the terrace
to swallow crunch-crunch
from head to wriggling tail

watches a warty gecko on the wall
the gecko on the wall
watching the cat on the ground

In the shade under the terrace
a young poet drinks our red wine
reads us his sheaf of typescripts

We praise the scent of almond blossom
and promise of summer

One day the Holy Family passes
Josephy walking
Mary and child on an ass

I greet them
with '*Adios!*' and a wave
across the *Cañada*

*Alhaurin el Grande (Málaga)*

Cañada de las Palomas: Ravine of the Pigeons Filomena: nightingale
mirador: view point pueblos:villages, small towns terraza: balcony
Adios!: Hullo!

# Jackie

The cold north wind
from her daughter's death
blew two thousand miles
to put the Bay of Biscay
France
and most of Spain
between her and the graveyard

Gibraltar and the Atlas mountains
framed in her window

Every night her red fox
crossed the Pyrenees
jumped the Channel
to paw the grave
and slept all day
his red brush wrapped round her brain

She moved from the Costa del Sol
from English sherry parties
in her luxury flat
from gossip by the bathing pool
to the *Andaluz campo*
and its whitewashed *pueblos*

Having bought her parcel of ground
from Juan's family
dowsed
and found a buried spring ·
she cleaned furnished and stocked
an old *casita*
with food and a full wine cask
first buying out a squatter peasant
and hiring him to grow her vegetables

Here
she would watch the rise of her new home

★      ★      ★

In our red car
we drove beyond the suburbs
following the route
they had told us at the Luna Bar
inland
to where the road dipped at the ford
dry after winter rains
parked
by Jackie's car
and walked the rough track
by the parched *arroyo*
into the wild *campo*
of bee orchids
blue pimpernels
bright irises out of the dry path
and the secret friar's cowl
green and purple
that flowers first
when the black almonds blossom


Would they ever lay a road
to Jackie's house?

'*Arriba!*'
shouted a peasant
and we found the *finca*

Jackie
washing the *paella* pan
in a pail
dried her hands

104

and drew white wine
from the cask

By chance we had come here
the first day water ran crystal
and liquid silver
and the seven men of Juan's family
tired
from the new well
and the square reservoir
had come for *comida*
under the reed canopy
their shirts flecked with
Andalucian sunshine

The old man
by custom
had laid three stones on the ground
in shape of a clover leaf
symbol of the Trinity
pushing three bundles
or dry twigs
between the stones
to focus the fire's heat
knowing by practice
when the *arroz con pollo*
was ready
the chicken tender
the rice unbroken
and lifted the sooty pan
on to the table

We served ourselves
from the common dish
our wineglasses filled
again and again
with cloudy wine from the cask

Juan lifted a scrap of chicken
from the pan
and dropped it on my plate
'*Carne!*' he said
with a smile
and we felt fully accepted
by his Spanish family

Then he showed us
his family's old *contijo*
with wooden olive press
cobwebbed and dusty

Returning
he broke off two branches
of white almond blossom
for Jackie and my wife

Once Jackie's new house was finished
they would sell
no more land
to be left with two mountains

'What can one make
of two mountains!'

       ★       ★       ★

Two years later
Jackie died
suddenly
like the man in the Bible
who built barns

campo: countryside pueblo: village casita: cottage arroyo: watercourse
Arriba!: Up! finca: rural holding paella: rice with chicken etc. comida:
lunch carne: meat contijo: farm ('j' pronounced as in lo*ch*)

## La Huerta Del Jorobado

The hunchback is buried in his name
here in the *Huerta*
where the little Scops owl
calls all night
twenty-two times every minute
in the pinetree by the dry reservoir
and the nightingales sing all day

The peasants throw their boots
to silence them

On our flat Moorish roof
I ease myself slowly
into a deckchair that scalds my back
and wonder why
Maria del Carmen's dog
Clarence
has left my chair in the shady porch
to climb the steps to this white roof

My hand tells me
our white roof is cold as iced water
and I learn at first hand
why all the *pueblos* yonder
across the campo to the far sierras
are white

My seat
in the afternoon heat of siesta
is here
under the pomegranate tree
in the corner
between our little house and the orchard
where I watch the civilization of the black ants

*Nispero* leaves fall heavily
from the trees

The church clock
in the white town above me
drops me the time hour by hour
and girls' singing games
from the school playground up there
till in the cool of late afternoon
from the orchard
the sound of milking the olive trees

but there are no olive trees in the orchard

I don my panama hat and dark glasses
walk the longer way through the orchard
and through the hole in the wall
broken by thieves
and there they are

a line of short trousers and knickers
draped along the top of the wall
and beyond the wall the long sticks beating

Behind them I stand still
till by chance a boy looks round
drops his stick to run
and one by one
they drop their sticks and run

I have said nothing
and return to the hole in the wall
where a woman with covered basket
stops

Fear in her eyes tells me
she knows that I know
what is in the basket on her arm

'*Buenas tardes*'
I say politely as I pass her

I give the same greeting to la Señora
widow of the Málaga judge
as she passes me under her sunshade

I know nothing of her late husband's judgments
under Franco
and have not questioned her daughter
whom I hear
giving Spanish lessons in their garden

        ★      ★      ★

Half-awake one morning
I dream of the Alhambra
beyond my closed eyelids

Water is running
dancing in fountains
in gardens
spouting from stone mouths
in the *Patio* of the Lions
and singing downhill to chill Granada

        ★      ★      ★

Beyond our night-shuttered windows
from somewhere
the one-day water is running
filling la Señora's reservoir

Two men in straw hats come
from somewhere
with mattocks
and outside our open windows
draw
wide as their mattock blades
little canals among their potatoes
and round the one tree of ripe oranges

Another day
a family comes from somewhere
first father and a mule with two panniers
and after school
mother with five children
to harvest the ripe *nisperos*
for their fruit stall in the *mercado municipal*

'I'll not be able to sell any more'
says father in his Andaluz dialect
flavoured with Moorish like his children's faces
and they go
father mother the five children
and the mule with full baskets
leaving half the orchard unharvested

We heap bowls and plates with yellow *nisperos*

★      ★      ★

One Sunday evening
Maria del Carmen
invites us to English tea and sweet cakes
she says she has fetched from Coin
specially for us

In the *salón* we congratulate la Señora
on the full success of her eye operation
She smiles behind tinted glasses
I kiss her hand

We join the family circle round the round table
the table-cloth by tradition down to the floor
drink tea
from antique cups dredged from Málaga harbour
and discuss the latest novels
and American films

The Alcalde's son
just come from Málaga
stands silent by the doorway
awaiting our eyes

'Picasso's dead!'
he says

I hear still
the silence in that room

*Alhaurin el Grande (Málaga)*

Le Huerta del Jorobado: The Orchard of the Hunchback. pueblo: village,
small (country) town campo: countryside sierra: mountain range
nispero: medlar milking the olive trees: beating the olive trees to gather
the fruit from mats on the ground Buenas tardes!: Good afternoon
patio: courtyard mercado municipal: town market Alcalde: Mayor

# VI

# Window On Edinburgh

Here
triptych windows frame the same sky
Sirius keeps his star timetable
the moon her months
the high trees their seasons
where the owl halloos and the grey squirrels play

Look!
in the first window-frame left
three and a quarter hundred million years
cast in lava
a grey lion couchant
focusses the long tenements' perspective

Between this window and that hill
a forest full of hartis hindis toddis
and siclike maner of beastis
dissolving resolving
imagined among suburbs
I zoom my lenses
from the forest forward through memory's
fourth dimension
focussing one house
at the end of the road to Kamchatka
where a lame poet taught a famed poet
a dead fact of no great significance

Yesterday a grey cat on the stone stair
up from a dark close with three prams
fled me through its own trapflap
in the unpainted door of an empty flat

★      ★      ★

From our mid window one century old
we view over the road four centuries
where bare-winter black and full summer
the trees' two seasons
reveal then veil in green a grey house
rebuilt on the white ashes of war
a shotgun wedding that misfired
four hundred and more years ago

No council has yet cancelled history
here
voting a final felling of the forest
cleaning the last patina from time's walls
bulldozing
scattering a stutter of prefabs
or towers of picture frames without pictures

Three pictures we bought with this house
and bought this room for the three pictures
linked like an altar-piece by the Master of Flémalle
the left wing a road to a dead volcano
the mid panel a house seen through trees

Gulls fly across the grey walls
and across
one on a gable's end on a corbie step
rests
and a still blackbird on a black brance
watches a bluetit delousing a twig

★    ★    ★

In the west-wing window a townscape
tenements of polished pewter at first dawn
windowed walls of scoured copper at sunrise and
by night lit windows suspended in darkness

By a stepped terrace of crow-stepped houses
white gulls float on the putting green
their painted bowsprits piercing the breeze

From blue slates
yellow chimney-pots and
steel aerials
a black pencil
from one of four churches at Holy Corner
aspires to high Heaven
which telescopes have pushed out of our universe

Remembering our first horizon
between seascape and skyscape
I paint and repaint Pompeian windows

The first
from Andalucia
frames Gibraltar
clear against the heat-haze of Africa

On the blue bay the black porpoises play

In Zermatt
in a cool hotel room
the maid pushing two window shutters
in blue sky frames the Matterhorn

On Vomero
high over hot white Naples
while Geppina stuffs aubergines
with minced meat rice and garlic
we view her kitchen vista to the blue bay and
in the heat-haze the twin of our gray lion

The fire in our Scots Vesuvius is out
In the house the ghost of the green lady
is doubly dead
At the road's end there's a black candle-snuffer
over a bleak kirk in the black night

★     ★     ★

But morning dawns from the black lion's mane
and our ears wake to the town's timetable

From the street the ring of horsehoofs on granite
glass on wire and a smashed milkbottle

A zinc pail dropped on the first landing
announces the once-a-week stairlady

A wrought-iron gate dinting iron
the loose latch to the street clinking shut
feet on the stair and our letter-box snapping
like a mousetrap delivers the morning mail
Japanese picture-stamps framing our names
and a New-Year letter from our niece in Naples

The sun makes on one wall a zodiac
light recreating pastel and painting
as on the first day of their creation

# Flodden

A hawk hovering over oak trees
I watch where
by footpaths and rutted road
an army moves
in a mad migration south
slow oxen pulling the great cannon

A King's red banner and the blue banners
of two saints
beyond the hills yonder
meet the bright banners of other saints
of another King
and there's civil war in Heaven

I follow the King who passed this way
who has no royal tomb
his bones thrown into
an old waste room among rubbish
his skull in another place among skulls
of other men's skeletons

They made a song of his army
whose dead were the fodder of the four horses
in the nightmare of John Surnameless

with Sword and with hunger and with death
and the beasts of the earth

# Lallan

*to Robert Garioch Sutherland*
*Poet*
(1909–1981)

Here in my third city
while the smoke of your burning
is in our nostrils
and your Lallan voice
still in our ears
I sit
here
where the two diagonals of the map
cross at this green place
where the flowers of the Drumselch Forest
have been trampled by millions of feet
to the grass roots

your book on my knee
with its dance of death

I will lodge you by Fergusson
and bid Burns lie
a little further
to make you a room

When our capital slept
and Parliament died
they came from the south
to divide our inheritance
giving Dunbar and Henryson
to Chaucer
and Burns to Oxbridge
for their histories of Eng. Litt.

A civil war of words began
words
that spread from a blot
on Shakespeare's manuscript
  'This sceptered isle
  this England'
and crossed the Border with Bible and bribery
vanguards of Empire
whose English army fought Napoleon
whose English army fought Hitler
where our nation has no name
a peninsula in the north end of England

From the second city in my memory
northward
I climbed Gaelic mountains
Cairn Toul Braeriach
Cairngorm Ben Macdhui
that speak no Gaelic now
and my grandmothers' maiden names
McNaught McConnell McNairn
recessive in marriage
died leaving me no Gaelic
as you few echoes from Sutherland

But in your death let me remember
my grandfather by the kitchen window
with horn spoon supping his porridge
with sour milk and salt
dreaming of Ayrshire
and
of another Robert
who seemed still a near neighbour
one from an ironstone mine
one from the same farmland

that bore my little grandmother
both neighbours of our name castle
both speaking your language
of the Garioch
(girnal of Aberdeenshire)
of the farms and oatfields of Scotland
of Glasgow closes
and wynds of Edinburgh
where another Robert wrote his poems

A long time before I was born
grandfather moved his family to Glasgow
to make his son a Greek scholar
and I son of a younger son
was born into my first city
where uncle taught me Latin
a dead language

But in three kitchens
three women
talked to us as women talk
to children
their rhymes and proverbs
flavouring their Lallan
like herbs

And later Scotland sang to me

Jeannie in Aberdeen and Belle
in Blairgowrie of the berry fields
singing without book or songsheet
their heirloom Lallan songs and ballads

The Arbroath fishwife who
collected songs and in her basket
wild flowers of the Angus glens
and the young women of Auchmithie
laughing
who swept me from house to house
without knocking
to listen together to
the centuries-old ballads
of their ancients

The thistle grows tall in Langholm
and in your poems
Edinburgh speaks again

A rare fellow
using your folly
like a stalking horse
to shoot the arrow of your wit
and wisdom

# Ufo

I held the lead pencil
by the blunt end
between left forefinger and thumb
and let the black ant run along it

Halfway I changed my grip
to the sharp end
between right forefinger and thumb

The short-sighted ant
gripped the blunt end
waved two antennae
into space
spiralled round the pencil
between blue sky
and no earth
and ran back along the pencil

Halfway I changed my grip
again to the blunt end

The ant stopped
at the sharp end
waved two antennae
into infinity
marooned on a green UFO in space

My pencil touched down
and the ant hurried off
to report her voyage
to where God shines by day

They added this happening
to the list
in the office of the Flying Ants

Talk between antennae
continued for weeks
whether God or the Devil
in the eleventh dimension
controlled these phenomena

*Prince Hamlet's Play-Within-the-Play*
a new interpretation from
*The Second Quarto*

*Subtle*   Was not all the knowledge
Of the Egyptians writ in Mystic symbols?
Speak not the Scriptures oft in parables?
Are not the choicest fables of the poets
That were the fountains, the first springs of wisdom,
Wrapped in perplexed allegories?

*The Alchemist* Ben Jonson

126

## Mr Shakespeare To Dr Dee

In Prince Hamlet's Play
let us begin with
the Aristophanic parabasis
where action stops
when Clown-Hamlet and his Queen
talk together

Here in my new Quarto
newly imprinted
in the year of the two stars
1604
the Clown-King and his Queen Gertrad
*Exeunt*

The Court watches Hamlet's empty stage

★      ★      ★

In the magic Mirror of imagination
Mummers enter
one with gilt crown
five with swords
dancing out of the dark
beyond the torches
where the recorders pipe
and Beelzebub the Ghost watches

The Clowns
weaving a fivefold Rose
collar their King's neck   .
in a ruff of swords
his crowned head
pilloried in a steel star
and where King Hamlet died in the Dumbshow

on the bank of flowers
Clown-Claudius falls
killed by the five swords of the Rose collar

Lay a Claudian cloak
over the corpse!

★        ★        ★

The serpent
hissing sin to Eve
in Eden

was King Hamlet's Ghost
on the battlements

was the Raven croaking 'Revenge!'
from the dark orchard
where
Hamlet's Clowns
have killed Clown Claudius

Hamlet's purpose
to catch the King's conscience
like the Duke in the last scene of
*As You Like It*
        His crown bequeathing ...
            and all their lands restored

Again
the five swords have danced in
from the dark
Five Clowns weave
a steel Star
not a death collar

a Rose
where Prince Hamlet
holds his sword-hilt
as a Cross
in the blank Centre
of the Sword-Rose
a Rosencross
as in the Centre of your Great Seal

A Mirror
held high
wherein King Claudius sees
the inmost part of him

In his nephew's magic Mirror
held up to Nature
King Claudius
had watched in the Dumbshow
his brother's death
and watched his own death
lying there
under his own cloak

Lucianus
kneeling by the Clown Claudius
drips his glass of air
in his dead ears

'A poysons him i'th Garden'
says Prince Hamlet
'for his estate'
but the dead Clown-King Claudius
rising
dances out with the five sword-dancers

renaisssance of the dead King
of the Waste Land
Denmark
cured from death by Lucian
Doctor of the dance
(Hamlet
who speaks the last words
of his own Play)

'You shall see anon
how the murtherer'
(nephew to the King
Lucianus
Hamlet)

'gets the love of Gonzago's wife'
(Queen Gertrad)
an eye for an eye and
a tooth for a tooth

'The King rises'
says Ophelia

'Give o'er the Play!
Lights! Lights! Lights!'
says Polonius

Claudius
born again
twice born
through the Devil-dark
flees from himself
in the Mirror

and Prince Hamlet
dances a jig
singing

'For if the King like not the Comedie
why then belike he likes it not perdy'

## Dr Dee To Mr Shakespeare

*Johphiel.* The company of the Rosy-cross you widgeon
The company of players.
*The Fortunate Isles and their Union*
Ben Jonson

From Denmark to far Bohemia
though not in London
your Play of Death and Resurrection
*Hamlet*
will go the Pilgrims' Ways
with the Players
travelling by road and footpaths
where Rosencreutz long ago
and I later
carved on trees
scratched on walls
stamped on men's minds
Rose and Cross
as once the Fish on walls of catacombs

Birds calling to birds of their own kind
in a medley of birdsong in thick forest
you send my Rose Cross
my Gold Star
in the names of two actors
Rosencraus and Guyldensterne
and a sword dance
that the Company of Travelling Players
may keep alive
through Europe
my invisible Company
of the Rosy Cross

In the year just past of your own *Hamlet*
in the year of the Two Stars
R.C.'s tomb
after 120 years
opened a door wide to Europe
and the Last Millenium

King James forgets I taught Mathematics
angles triangles but remembers only my Pentangle
not for but against witchcraft
that I talked maps with Mercator taught Frobisher
Drake Hawkins Gilbert and Davis navigation
angles that opened up Atlantis and the world

Broken I go no more oversees
to guide the Second Reformation now in Europe
but sell my bound books to buy bread

I saw my library scattered my many manuscripts
torn to wrap cakes or light fires

But talk to me again of your later plays
budding to flower one by one in your mind
of the last of your sons
not like the failed Hamlet
who lacked magic to overpower King
and Devil
but a Magus
Prospero
with Book and spirits to command
that the man I might have been but am not
be resurrected from script or Quarto in words
and action to be my immortality
that someone in the far future may again find me